Pangs!   Robert Herbert McClean

AF083686

1.0

The facilitator is high on life. I- is not real. This is the closest thing I'd to sex- ~~year after sexy year. A phoney moralist took photos of girls gone wild for kink without asking permission.~~ I sing complimentary lo-fi arias- I tinkle our *Supertone* piano- as if I is abandoned on an autobahn. Travelling ~~say 200 K per hour~~ obfuscates this status quo. ~~If you travel-~~ I found myself ~~travelling-~~ where and when there is always tea in the pot. ~~Pause for clichéd flies enchanting a stunt corpse.~~ I'm unwilling to concede- ~~for now.~~ When you laugh at my computer software manual- ~~I touch myself like no goon recorded.~~ Method based on hunch. The weight of your world ~~already~~ haunches ~~your affable/laughable shoulders.~~ I polemically challenge sexism at a urinal with a boob tubed gent pissing. Yoked it to chunder. ~~Status- I gripe and bemoan which~~ with the fond gripe I know the one with the two roads. Unashamedly cool he deftly removes his digit from my sphincter. 666 it reads scrawled in blood- bolstering the annex of the poem to the poet. ~~Go and~~ study it where everything is- in the wild play of god- ~~and not on my laptop.~~

1.1

Nothing I seem. ~~She came out tetchy in a towel.~~ ~~You'll never learn to~~ speak with a brogue- ~~that Poplar whispers~~ from the bog bank. Eat that ~~therapeutic cheese burger- ready to take on this~~ world with ideas/words. In bed I composed ~~I supposed for/from-~~ a magnanimous skit ~~in the metropolis. Straw strewn all over our shared carriageway~~ of combusted corpses. A lush drag queen playful with a shy stag- perpetually sneezes his dysmorphic body weight. He clambered into an uprightish stance- tittering ~~of open waters deep and~~ with a well proportioned yes. ~~For this orange summer seemed unusual to linger.~~ Rapture is long late my cowardly darling- so… ~~The black puppy has so much empathy- it finds~~ my once peachy girlfriend is said to be an *It Girl* ~~to two pished mini-skirted boob tubed yahoos.~~ ~~Me~~ tattooing you on my arm- ~~eating out~~ my spazzy ~~cousin twice removed. This was~~ fleeting ~~and I~~ was not becoming- ~~but~~ already assuaged by ghostly truth always here in the apparency of space in a continuous monotonous dirge- ~~I don't want to watch *iPlayer*/*Netflix* or *LOVEFiLM*. All roads lead out. All roads lead home-~~ e.g. We're transcribing an irrefutable language.

1.2

You- my dear- I've been. ~~And then~~ she sighed ~~and said no- let's get up- and why is?~~
Imagine your father figure ~~before heaven's gate- his body's last expulsion. Disaffected &...~~
My economic dinge is spectral. ~~Penny guff split pavement chunks.~~ She fox-trotted
her figurative frame forwards. Your moronic contempt ~~for the "Yeooohhh!" crew~~
has been bureaucratically noted. ~~Entrance like for a bomb shelter or bi-plane hangar.
Deafeningly loud,~~ skeleton reaper shook bones in synch. Encounter 500 kilos exploding
from a lorry load of haystacks. Either my leg or foot or these brakes aren't working preferably.
I'll conflate disguised as a domestic bather ~~behind chub lock- the classic noise of a river~~
where we stood- as if only survivors. ~~By God and friend by foe or fellow man? Find out who.
What. What goes. In the whir of the chugging motor.~~ Thought of the fire between your legs
raises suspicions. Links I like- I post on *Facebook* about David Graeber. I asked her to explain
if she could- plainly, to barter balances of flowering vapours.

1.3

She quivers- or says she quivers- yes- lots of yes- caresses my balls and cudgel.
We claimed a right to declare ourselves citizens in the call of fault lines. Catch my drift?
"Semiotics sucks." Lover get loose. ~~I loved you but gave up trying love.~~
Behind that musty velveteen drape. ~~You roll your eyes and reach.~~ Your *Jehovah*
superglued petulant subwoofer headphones to your ears. Whisper ~~to shake under the bed beside me and~~ be quiet- very quiet. The boy asked who/~~why(?)~~ were paramilitaries
shedding for something consistently disputable. In a calculated shower of shrapnel
somebody in the interim of bang! Stalwartly I don't apply and concutate. Rumour has it-
a cancerous yokel monopolized these pastures- or in favour of her grump-
~~she took a hot bath~~ to cool off Christianity's acid cud- chewed over smoked soap-
a pot of kratom tea- to see what way you see the world. ~~Fair game?~~ Fucker.

1.4

This important poet to be & I- bathed once a week at a hippy chick's flat in Le Marais.
I'm the birthplace of every surrender. The tribe's sacred cow. An epic haiku scribbled
to drown dead centre. The stars- yes. With lease of life- this life at least- at last.
A ballet dancer- in this current context messes spacetime fuckery- stays a while on
celebratory tour- in a cranial denouement- in the metropolis of gilded streets.
Shocked bodies shunting for position. She lost her towel in the scuffle
twice a day. In a sumo suit I burst whomever I choose- while my panging nerves quibble
with what is real. You can tell a lot by the photographs posted online of the girls gone wild.
Like sprung swallows bashfully swoon for you- like the speckled dizziness you oddly trust-
that talks- cooks- and keeps a good lookout with a dermatologist who specializes in moles.

1.5

When we're ancient finally like interdependent- I'm stillness- in shifting sands that end all deserts. Bulb sticky- I blow my holographic self. We can fall asleep in our chairs we can. Hey you- in my defence- imagine my mind a limitless space in which you wittingly levitate. Your arbitrary sentence structure is beguiling at best. You're a linguistic floozy.
You're like a car bomb. I mean everything. I desire pure sex in which I can't hear clear the oceans- due wilting into bursting. Like little flames set so under fibre-optic lights.

1.6

Give thanks for raw tutelage. Purchase a banana to gutcomfort. An imitation dies.
I can hear faint... "What gives you the right to be so cute? Huh?" I caress my bad self.

1.7

For a piebald one liner- who'll dog you in a *McDonald's* car park? I can understand you thinking my bed belches like an insidious black hole in my slumberchamber. I feel debauched- dear God- I'll drown removers of lives once lived- lived out. My friend- with regards current situation. Fool. He's issues- he brings them pent to shoot- in and of whatever this world- open wide- left wanting. More complicated- seriously- resembles girls gone wild at a formal- conferring over someone with the voice of a dying gull- who got fatter writing this on nothing but words- with a dose of haemorrhoids. In the indentation of my brow's furrow- I is crazier than kids on prescription drugs. Like most I took up religion since my last confession- was way way existentialist.

1.8

I'll put money on your Doldrums- and I can tell you that you will make a long journey
and you will see your companion is an Uncle who thinks you queer- and he says if
your lover ever hides her passport- politely talk to the authorities- so for me he's steadfast
as a bastard- or the Pleiadians- or even Carl Sagan. I took a scrap of paper from my pocket
along with a pen- and like falling in love on my final breath in a patriotic heave- I bore
the brunt of defence and boundary- and write- *you've made me a pauper in the heart*.
My potential mate approaches hands folded- like hovering- she wears nothing else
but red lipstick- dictatorially describing the scene. Turbines thrash thin air- spark electricity.
In her lush glory she strode in erotic spiritoso. On fire- my love likes to wear black
in memory and in honour of bad taste- begun against the drooping sun in its easterly sway.

A cynic's dog is innocent in dream. Person versus place- unified forever fresh like with a non stop pout. Let's Forge- Cyborg- strung out on SSRI- unable to punk or recognize how I looked at me like I'd no choice- like both futures now dependent on incalculable affection. All is as you said it seems- I'm destitute- funnily destroyed by some sinister careers advisor- in the flushes of a toilet- while religiously pining for a good Samaritan's ear- and a rare filet mignon. ~~Slick pauper~~ life is not a box of prospects.

1.10

She poses life as a soap opera- and she poses for the rich douchebag she is tasting. She looked at him sweat some- then they fucked- hard. I'm the gash for every wab- she said. I'm a spacetime cartographer- dumbass- he said. When you click me out of this iniquity- this intensity of everything I won't give up- for when she spat my sour load from our sofa- it crumped becoming debris from a suspect device- and I unfurled- unfulfilled.

1.11

Do ~~or don't you know~~ what a bomb sounds like? Outside the clique of teenage pregnancies.
If I could herd the crooked ~~bullocks my pores would seethe~~ humdrum airs. ~~Equestrians~~
I'm a crannog where alt-poets commit suicide. Yo! This subjective ebb is no fun.
Only told your truth when you said you didn't believe in ownership but lied when you said vomit
rises/subsides in my oesophagus. ~~Colour of this weather has you all embarrassed at menstrual staining whomever's mattress- sputtered with tongue laid in ice-cream.~~ The technological flair
won't go on forever- ~~like eating with your hands- abandoned mitres-~~ a suggested trademark.

1.12

She text she was sorry my eloquence is beyond translation- no strings attached
or boyfriends- no sad slow husbands- stupefied yet mesmerized by this banal wit.
She sympathetically sighed with giddy aplomb. Honestly- we are all children of God
whether this was a good idea at all. The strangest heart I've ever known hopes
you've no bombs in your pockets. He's pure romantic- I cried like a wimp to be so lucky.

1.13

The inn sold no antitoxins- only export stouts. I- musters mumbles- M.I.A. I- dances resembling a delirious stork- pukes banana bile at rusty gates of Presbyterian Churches. You're quite a diabolical badass- a quantum menace. Your essence seduces a tamed serpent- a translucent python adorned on the shoulders of my doppelgänger- who danders google maps- getting shit seen to. I- flutters like a tripping bird in the grip of a psychopathic poacher in tweed- who repetitively said something incomprehensible about Sauerkraut. Ask Me for rolly papers at squat parties. I don't want to move to Berlin. Lamentable- the boyfriend beater- perhaps in a linen frock a la mode- to watch a movie- then her desire flexed her atoms on a charity shop sofa that is patchy sticky after the pornomoronathon. The party of fear and guilt is in full swing of forgetfulness. I lay a bandy kneed beauty therapist for hot blood.

1.14

Inside I'm crimping. My loose teeth chomp- I slip the current. I fibbed about the demon of the black hound- you Know? The ole third *Anti-Christ* rises- the final fall of Rome. Newsagents' windows glistened under street lamps shattered. Warped Science or eventual demise. Jackdaws cuckaw for summer dusk over fields- raging for bonfires.

1.15

You took a hatchet to someone who took umbrage to a Union Jack. I want you in the room- whichever room to breathe of a stranger. A politician's sprog decides- yes- dinosaur deniers are certifiable- but will be saved by premonitory whimsy- AKA John the Revelator. A *Tour Guide* gaunched- somewhere- a bin bag of buried ecstasy tablets. To the wind he's shown skulk of retro- through merciless defeat of happenstance- stardust rebelling again.

1.16

A paramilitary hero's attempt to pipe bomb civil servants is considered Performance Art.
So what if the wardrobe stinks of damp- usually well repressed- profusely in fact- for periods.
The tabloid supplement contained paramilitary funeral photos circa 1992. A man in a cloak
in the district- he'll accept the ranch hand job offer if- a bomb explodes in a shopping mall.
Buckled behind walls of tennis courts is an ape on holiday- homesick for sexual captivity.
A mutant Alsatian howled at the full main moon attempting to hide amid brackish clouds.
In this camouflage malaise I re-imagine my comforting thoughts- conjugated by my self.
So I said this is the town wherein if you close your eyes to everyone you disappear-
computer cowboy- in a concentrated cacophonic smithy. Nitrate or manure. Either Or.
I explore in mirth sorts.

1.17

Prototype workplace bully- she bites the boiled eggs marking the malodorous grave.
I'm insecure- outsider- glib gab- heavenly inaccuracies save fallibility of sin.
All apocope convos- less hapless- homeward bound- we worshipped people dying here.
I'm chipping buzzard bones- highly praised in moonlight blue. The learning curve
could be averted with the dribs of her drabs- in a panicked e-dreamscape. You've the face
of a doe-eyed altar boy. My love sprouts from the pips of your dowry. I've grown
a comedy moustache for my own bathetic reasons. Darling- should I go speed dating?
Sanctimoniously brave- I dare not dither. I ingested an incy thumbnail ace of spades.

1.18

Of our gifts to give this world- I double took digital hands- shook fierce on Stormont steps. For this scatological farce we sing slovenly- pure pop ballads. I was taken out and shot through the heart. At ease is interrupted by laughter. Farts. On top of a washing machine in shift- with nothing to sell- scriptless- feeling no need for energy drinks or last rites- I require a bouncer to chuck me out of the hipster fray. Soldiers swept cribs out onto frozen loughs because they were honest in proclaiming we're mythic birds colliding in a predatory scuffle. Watch reality TV and ignore my sweet paunch. Friends- loves- affiliates- after after I feel for the flow? Or so goes the story? I cupped my balls artistically- represented my flaccid cock on foolscap. Soft porn is projected on the screen of the sore sky. Use this sort of service 24/7. If I fell in love here- I escort. He takes his pistol off the wardrobe- checks it's loaded- and then asks for you- sure as death- you didn't believe in slurps of passion- or me as the gelding grazing on magic mushrooms. I thought how I think I'm promises- how the hangman's parties are over.

1.19

Have you any experience with 500lb of debris and flames? A week exact before Marjorie Pope. These men creep our driveway like black holes do the galaxies. Within a wall of mirrors the sky was chalk. I slugged a quart of whisky on our balcony like a desperate recluse- enough proof to decipher your deluge. Pucker up but refrain the unsmooched figment. You will if beyond reasonable doubt you've more sense still than money. I'm not going to write any more poems to appease weirdo extras who loiter with a strict curfew- in love scenes I direct lucid dreaming.

1.20

Well educated. Ultimately unemployable. I consciously liked disliking him with some success- composed a shopping list treatise on the I love you subject- in a gnostic fume.

1.21

Internal dingleberry defo. No cock cancer. Made puerile flesh and bone. A shrewd/just leader who's also in the dole queue. We've seen ~~blood red hands as~~ a super volcano happening. This golden history is about ambivalence to the image. Bruise these stunk foot schemes with a diligent kiss- the dirt of future in-laws. Convince me of the concept stuck in your cajoled skull- that hearts are much like eggs. A grace she obliged to spin light my bum note yarn.

1.22

To my intolerant ears he explained his digitally restored photographs of Hollywood starlets. I asked him to articulate his anger as a sadomasochist in a shrunken tank top who'd caught scabies. I love you like stew. Eat stew- you atomic thing. You're mad to think I'll apologise in advance for this apophatic rant. He's disappointed these feelings aren't mutually exclusive. The fish bowl on his head didn't make him an astronaut when I butterfly kissed the Friesian snout.

1.23

2.0

I'm ~~much like the feral fox from~~ a ~~no place like home- or the~~ singing donkey to native cochleas. ~~A father figure in a police uniform carrying a coffin of limbs only- open eyed. Regurgitated lentils~~ stain this porcelain bowl I flush- along with a part of myself- mildly exonerated. I twiddle my thumbs as if in a Eucharistic time lapse. Is it all about the abstract or an exam to pass? The learning curve could be averted with the pristine dribs of her drabs.

2.1

I want to lick the insides of your upper arms as a careering humanist. You're the beauty that makes a lazy eye spook. She sent me a pair of her lace panties- forgive her- believe her when she says you're a miscellaneous resolution. I probably got this voice from a movie I saw.

2.2

Fond bends ~~of the bob and tug~~ of love ~~giving over~~ as if ~~an illegal~~ fireworks display. Swans are the best friends of a shoe seller's ghost. I told her she's the coldest witch of any winter. The litany of the spoilt is harrowing. She's as warned- a strange- beautiful affliction- a darling who can die and die- as you taunt the caustic sun- tweeting impacts- banished in a bonus level.

2.3

She was too afraid to challenge the scepticism of Schopenhauer- popping pills in Amsterdam. I'd a one night stand there like being buried alive with the remains of your retarded captors. The orange bud begged belief in smoke. This everything I want it to be. Yes- the Irish sea is a tryst and we're tricked as penance for fly tipping church wreckage into a turquoise calm. We entertain other quackish pop philosophers who watch a plasma flat screen to dismiss the poetic. I'd feel awful- ask you if you want to have costumed sex- to say you want to is a lie.

2.4

Led by a psychopath in red high heels- your paltry ghost spends too much time in the shadow of a draft text message- assured by me- access should be trusted and weigh heavy on a mind- to later wade through in a hallowed dark with a hallowed name- or a sorry for your troubles. Real life- forgive me. I've not sinned- for you're a voice for burnt ears- a child's balloon. The traffic lights are haywire- like an unassembled jigsaw- or dandruff- or the daily news. I'm the foetus of every abortion. You aren't going to believe this- but I'm thinking of the sea- tasting of vomit- I'm a lover offering semblances of happy- in a chic strip club's basement.

2.5

I'm textually debunked. You still think I'm the apple of your eye? I'm stood in my pyjamas in the dole queue. I scream thrash metal spirituals- dagger clad- willing bombastic to defend my offspring on social media. Sometimes your ghost speaks but we can't make out if- for all intents and purposes- she's a friend of Jesus. Such is life- she's my one conclusive trope. I celebrate cunnilingus freaks. My lips gift your face of songs. I purse them. Sexy. Real sexy.

2.6

From each consecutive moment there is the relevant intelligence. I was so drunk not for kinks of sex but due to a various illness. I saw no value in anything after fine dining tutorials and reprimands over hot conversation about poems. Lucky you're inspiration and I'm a weakling of pure intention with no fixed abode. Like cyber babes I heart your invasiveness- of the grip.

2.7

My cowardice is an indispensable luxury. I'm a muscle toned lugger. I blog the bones of it-
a sex slave in a vacuous expanse. I'm a credit check drought when the peelers raid the dealers.
My bum cheeks quiver in this dull freeze. I need money to buy stuff like Class A's or C's.
I've temporarily succumbed to theories ignored by totally fractured randoms. To achieve anything
other in unenjambed lines- like a pre-programmed country song in a discordant key- I give you
back your freedom idea in extremes. I'm famished from hunting treasure- i.e. a really funny
mime that I'll try to skit in a thrift store tizz with a stiffy- gurgling like a radio sinking in bath water.
So Poetry- what is it exactly? It was only after our shared dopamine surge we both realized.

2.8

When you laughed at said spiel I'd to graffiti my pseudonym on your ~~perky tits~~ with red lipstick.
When you rested your laptop on your gut you tried to guilt trip me into gushing your cunt
of the schism of love- its blunt release- you look like an events organizer for a fashion magazine.

2.9

I don't want to research conspiracy theories while we await fresh meat to join in line. An approximate value of this heart can tip the scales of sentimentality. My quotidian love is a raw egg. I'm so much fun for a poet ~~it hurts.~~ I hope to know someday what your love kinda was- with its gluey lubricant- like semi-precious tears. I want us both to understand what poetry negates ownership- but/or there must be more to life. You think? Like a considered prophetic truth? Call me chicken. She's my frump- my unfortunate vice. Do not be entranced by his candour of man and myth- for the sky is peach on the precipice of our salacious hormones. So long ~~bitches~~- props for conscientiousness. The whole universe hums- not even.

2.10

On the first day after the flood you conduct lightning with your pinkies. As my eczema peaked I lost my appetite for crunk. You didn't shoot yourself through the temple. My love is dopey cute when I procure her goofy dimensions on google. Paint your toenails- feeling mad wack in tiger print pyjamas- about the metaphor of who works the overhead projector. We contort in a chasm of fuck where everyone is really quite gentle. I'm 99.9 % sure I'll probably try to suffocate myself with your pillow or spurt a splurge of mercurial pulses on my duvet- substantially medicated.

2.11

Get to work to get God into your poem I guess? He is obviously pretty pissed about something.
Everywhere in everything and all at once. I'm anything if human- being an excerpt from
a virtual reality bang- which makes you smitten in mutual smirk and my personal favourite.
Someday you'll be able to speak in tongues and recite a poem based on bad habits and make
do with the salvaged gore in the scarce plunder. My extraordinary love is writing this poem.

2.12

Legs clamp legs. The whole room is a telephone ring- an adolescent celebrity's hyper dream- in which it looked like you were inside me on a sofa that savours my chump- and spits him another dreamy poem. Enough is enough of I. Anyone for a plate of scrambled eggs? My love is a panic button- a code you crack in her anxiolytic grip. Her climactic deft lick decreed a heart I fail to ignore with my variant array of tenderness. But we both know I've moved on from that- yet remain close enough to weep at her digital effigy. Heavenly- I mulled aghast- teeth grinding- quantifying each risk. Rehearsals start when I learn my few lines and find the detonator remote.

2.13

Read this book of Revelations without God. Learn to speak cow and pig- a dead language so beautiful like the sun on heights- only in that it is forever changing. Blown to bits and pieces- lack now their once precise physicality. In the end he got very difficult to all but me swollen with lust and love. Hey girl with the flaxen hair- mortified by and in his papal silhouette- don't take jibes too much to heart. I imagine you walking into every room I'm in- like a need. I'm a sardine in a can of sardines. If you break for no reason being on the brink be blown to support either/or waning cause of paradoxical meh. I will leave this sink in piss- these sheets in my new lover's blood- reading your poem aloud for fun with a multitude of voices- like a troupe of back to work actors who breached security. I bumble at the heist of the spectrum- charting stars- whose constellations look like pictorial dot to dots of us fucking in every possible position.

2.14

I want to smash my mobile phone as is always the way in whatever season- with feigned embarrassment and in such trying times- and in such trying times. Prime me baby.

2.15

His frustration led me to witness him wield a hatchet in a choreographed swoon. The irony inherent I suppose- I'm not by this stage salvaged. Your self is getting your hopes up about a brazen hussy. We were quite the misfits. Pell-mell I rested my free reign. We are fed and watered well. We took sledgehammer turns as earthling destroyers- drinking fruit smoothies- hungover. My love is not caring- not being held to account by the phantoms of facts. Surrender to germs in lungs. Kiss me with a purse like how a goldfish breathes- how I wrote this poem. Some dare to touch my sun burn now the parties are over. For a damsel for whom you'd gather flowers, for your favourite TV show- my brains are pewtered. Suits me- embrace it- punk.

2.16

For my ear lobes which you smooth with your thumbs- you mention like a precocious saint who shaved her head- your areolas can be read like a radar of the cosmos. I taste acidic and lack a crisis. I was just thinking about your bank balance and endangered species. I understand it is more than the sea and a rushing hand on a torso. All this complicates more so what to choose for breakfast. Out of the bare chug I just didn't get ~~my~~ love- I guess.

2.17

Panic in the blood to put these parts together. I love her in the knowledge I won't incorporate sharing a succession of moments- for she reads far too much for her own good. She showed orgasmic mimes with sums of her sporadic hippocampus- which reminds me of terminal cancer- how the unclassified universe abruptly closes- like a sphincter after a fart. I turned off the TV to confront history's immediacy in a fertilizer boom. I've given up trying to relax- it's saccharine.

2.18

Unconsummated love both our futures depended on. ~~I suppose~~ I like the scent of her gash as quotidian verses drone- she needs me to do it the way- say no ex ever did. Be my electricity. Feed my eccentricity in ballet slippers. Render us both champions- narcotic and good for blood- our hearts mended the troublesome confines of our love. I present my mitts. Breathe- she said.

2.19

With homeless crackheads- I'm charmed by your calm reserve- your casual strength of opinion- the militancy of your followers. I answered with a hard kiss- a tumble of the palm- the subject? I mean- I feel fragmented- but I know children of the future say something stupid below the belt to bogle me- as a vain locum laughs- as morning's solar flares stun painted ladies- like *Valium*.

2.20

A denim dress open at the chest spontaneously combusts. I consulted my oracle via real time fibre-optic. Blame me for introducing him to verse. I offer what I could with a limp shoulder like a man shot to slide down a blank wall simply for a decoration of blood. Doped pupils in a luminous dementia. I've confidence in the mental capacities of whoever auspiciously reads my warped poems except for the guy playing the real me. My love tells the debt collectors about those darling buds of kush- the tonic wine- the loneliness of drumlins devastates the voice.

2.21

I've held up walls on MDMA musing why someone put a bomb under your car for some other organization. A renowned drug dealer bound in a gimp suit- duct taped in a sleeping bag for matters of life and death. A hunky chauvinist. His skin was falling off- he gave me his business card- a pack of condoms.

2.22

Your memory is glitched by the romantic void in a carnal climacteric on her fishnets. It's a shame you look like being a confirmation- but muse- you're dead to me. My testimony is a bawl in riposte of everlasting doom- and out and out love. I was wrong to cum speechless in the ceremony of twice the effort. Her milkshakes would bring all the boys to the yard- account for natural disasters- global terrorism- blood money laundered. Eyes agaze- quiz me about love- let me tend your quim in places I saw not only in dreams but in the briskness of a thought before a thought. Lance the sun with a scalpel you fool- like it's your full time job. I'm a phallic thing that seeks wet refuge. A safety measure for the ensuing squall.

2.23

3.0

Have a goody bag- wet eyes. Tell me that you'd die for me. Come back to party when I get paid. I'll juggle two hearts for minimum wage. You might have a beautiful mind, but in the artificial dark you're a non sequitur- a chaotic hoax. For you- my best metaphors remain inorganic- password locked- and stored on my hard drive- for the bored altogether.

3.1

My love pinches my pink gloss of a form ~~a world away~~. Kiss me on the forehead like a sweetened drunk. Please- make the hair on my crown grow back. Get over yourself as unbelievable. Nobody benefits this stasis awry. I've signed an epitaph on a shocking pink *Post-It Note* in varying degrees of drunkenness. I'm on your level automatically tuned to portents. I'm the king of every jar of honey. Life is too short and chung. We only think we should believe we're in some sort of love like poetry. Your servants helped me escape. Kinship breaks both your legs. Your skulk is pure smut. She makes me feel like my knees are my elbows. I'm cold calling the sublime. We perform for audiences on CCTV- like merging fires. The only real conspiracy.

3.2

We've dizzy plans. We're insanely prepared with lipstick. The critical ecstasy of pink diamonds swank. Flutter your lashes in my bubble bath. Fill my quota of screwball witticisms. Give me a pregnancy scare. You look like someone I could introduce to my dead parents. The sky is CGI. Spiritualistic pimp- purge the spoils of choice in heavy thunder. I've been hand picked to play my own worst enemy in the poem- but you're trashy cute and downloadable like a torrent. I've powers once unknown that punk the vital imagination upon which we preach- mildly fascinated in derelict libraries. I'm allure from poppers on a porno set. I destroyed my weekend with your tinkering evocations. I would rather be in love than in a relationship- in order to blossom.

3.3

This song of praise goes on for a forever. I hypothesize the same for pseudo-romantic relationships. Look- she says- at the dumb pornography- there's plenty ideas to burn but no solid common sense. Lose your sanity in the brevity of a sneeze- begrudgingly start all over as a maniacal evangelist. Amateur dramatists sing *Edelweiss* on the shorelines of sweethearts- which reminds me of the shotter who spots blueys- and how you should wipe your feet on your way in and out- and hold your applause like a perfunctory second nature.

3.4

Iconoclastic- ~~dolled~~ in a dressing gown- squalor proud- you've fed the sentimental fool enough guff. A man who can decree with confidence a hobbyist's rhapsody- a scundered glory. A dote- my love- my love is a hand to pet ~~this fallower mind.~~ A brave rabbit scopes the well trod corral as I try to write better poems that maybe outlast a gamut of if without resignation to yes. By calling herself *Bad Luck*- her demure seduction technique was intangibly stricken of tactic- is frankly unnecessary- but no matter we're all monkeys- I look at all the monkeys with her tongue between my teeth- for webcams. She rated my life was way more beautiful.

3.5

They all wear balaclavas- black leather jackets and jeans. Like evil T-Birds. They belt towards the heavens he was a scourge- as she spruced my frisson with *Kleenex*. Tearily mock the moon you rabble at. I'm pretending to be a mute to dash commitment- or big words like commitment. I was fine dined by the director- she's promised to flash me on *Skype* and occupy my boredom. I think she has fallen a little in love. I'm hip to how it is to be young and rebellious with crackpot plans for weekends. I'm musically barren- I've nothing but the pressure of a market strategy- like a downer I opened my wallet to paw her surplus passport photo- delicately with hands that pretend to be interested in the bodies of others- that mutate into the ugly- the strangers in ourselves touch you like I'm happens in a flux of re-occurring.

3.6

I'm sorry I can't do this any more- I'm no cross-eyed- latex-gloved- renal consultant who will be your spouse- want you to raise their mixed up offspring. A Hawaiian pizza gave me bouts of diarrhoea when we were on *Skype*. Sometimes I've to ask which sorts of poems must not be compulsions. I'm discouraging *me* in a convex mirror dressed as a goth- shot through the heart with a bad dream. Behind the scenes of an interlude- crunk my chunk in your casual attire. Fighting social injustices entangled in my inability to kip- I pray. You think you can teach me wild abandon in pop socks while I crunch my maw?

3.7

You're more than the sum of websites. You're a pin up for an Anti-War demo who sweats the pressure of lyric convention I instinctively dodged. He told us he wrote emails to US troops in Iraq- to be indifferent to the plague of necessities and jokes because he was not foolhardy- or from the town- he did not lift the weights- he did not drink the wine. There are lots of randy divorcees on *Citalopram*. I held my breath besotted as I admired your fine features- stiff dicked- sweet toothed- a stone heavier- from a distance too far to defeat for a woman with two heads and two hearts. What I wouldn't give to kiss her midriff- on steroids- as a gangsta- her saying is that all puny geek gonna just drool? Her saying we could be commuting- organic agrarians.

3.8

I haven't shaved or brushed my teeth to join the resistance. I looked at myself poorly wrestle my flaccid member like it's a sedated- rabid dog. I pull the queasy faces of a lonely trespasser because the world was too much to confide in whole. I'm a moon affected by the tides. I relax-controlled in perfectly timed intervals of the fug of fingers/thumbs and tongue. I astutely followed cartoonish orders- petrified by the indigenous yarn of charmless loins- in our uncivilized infinity.

3.9

I want to eat out of your mouth- something like a fire. Blow me a kiss from the feeble hand of your geriatric father. With all your might grapple a die- let's tussle solipsism. I was merry on the ardour of her pits. I guffaw to strike a deal with the muse. With claw I've straggled. Stranded- I'd have to reconsider everything like literary classics- lackadaisical erudition. The internet death clock informed me alterity is abound. An absolute vice- as one precariously treads the far reaches of transgression- with an impervious fragment of what I once meant in bloom. Badly disturbed wearing your gown of organic wool- unsurprised by your ancestors who thought a hollow mind stranger- you're yet ultimately more delicate and concrete. Don't believe a word off my bookshelves for a totalitarian regime in this war of good versus evil. The genocide of dogs is torturous as the honey dew laps the tip of my heaven- sitting at a river in the countryside- pretending you're buddha on temazepam. Tell them you were held hostage. I can hide you- at best sit here until the light fades- enforce your anti-thesis firmly. With invisible prey ticket sales would plummet moot kerrangs- medieval sagas of love. His clumsy diligence is too funny and yet he is all smiles for hard labour. One of the company questions the answers as to what the weird poem meant. I step invisible out of my atomic rejuvenation for unruly painted ladies. I'd theories of my own. I balance now pretty good and portray sex through the spare dark. I can see from the border compound we're both bleeding. She has such awful teeth- hair like scorched flax. I should've bucked her when love sang a skewed idyll in my trousers. My love does not like porn if life is like a dream in eleven dimensions. I understand why you don't like to be alone. It was informative- transient almost- the first time. Dance to synth pop. I stave the giggle swell.

3.10

Immediately shushed about mortality ~~and Cindy Crawford's face.~~ It's the sublime of the duped Gael that syntactically shatters your mandible wet with woe- testament to the terror I know too well. You wouldn't have a gun I could borrow for profiteering in our abandonment? After which I did pine as a poet getting out of a toxic relationship. In a one windowed vacant room I'd time to remain unsmudged. As their mission begins another bomb explodes and we make this love finally hurl in overgrown country gardens- sunkist till one dies a bookslut- shuffling blindfolded- massaging knees into tough muck. I trust I'm a vested interest in her skits- each word a grail.

3.11

The stars seem unfettered by tempered minds on *Skype* and I think she is seriously serious about phantasmal fluorescent Gods. There are lots of single mothers on benefits beginning to crack. Retaining their self worth they make it clear that an immaterial- necessary journey- through a sunflower field of unaffected air- flexing- faultless- precipitates my role play as a cult leader- lushly intoxicated by the white mist and the thrill. The lewd spoof of a skewed idyll.

3.12

Everyone online is an artist these days. Gazumped ~~under an *Armitage Shanks* sink~~ I feel free to empty grace- play dead- spun in ~~the loom of~~ a dream. An armistice of blatant promises of the casual/virtual. There has been an insurgency. I leaked info- importune- the advice of a rigged tarot. I'm late for appointments because you're nervous of your taste and shape. With all its goading symbolism- my lean presence- an impromptu ruse for after an afterthought that raises questions- for your nobody in particular- spikes the seldom sensed glitch. As one gregariously laughs at me writing on their profile- I'm inundated with more to compose. If my love stretches your dimples- choose it. You've the most beautiful eyes.

3.13

Twinkle Noise- I grit my teeth and get tore in- ~~as a practising druid. For their ears~~ with that strange look- I scorn my propaganda in a false past- summoning deities for straight science. For poetry- it's like I can't toss a coin or get myself a flat with a washing machine. My love glimmers like a dream machine's in *YouTube* tutorials. I respond with tweets about toned abs- about romance- about the punctum of my self portrait. Some sense of a pastoral with yet another prospective employer. To forgive drunkenness I bite my fist- think it unwise- urged with a stare much like a wall. The bones of it blogged- my futile man mess- encouraging me.

3.14

Trust the kinetic intricacies of the dumbass who should've fingered you as you jittered for when you were on the phone with a rough failure- who gave everything he had away which cerebrally sprung a reminiscence- dib dabbing psychedelic lottery tickets- procured from a crusty in the valley of death. When you were stolen from spring she blew a tassle of split ends from her cheek- and told us we needed modernist haircuts- moisturiser- more veritable sunlight entrenched in the non-hazardous gulf between daytime TV and the famine. Love spewed a brutal wow out of the bare chug- I fantasized about you when I peaked- feckless in the vague emptiness of an epic fail. A myriad of me inconclusively indistinct- vibrates your choreographing eyes in multiple orgasms. Then I drink a gargantuan beer.

3.15

Out into the falsity of a moonlit silence- like some dream I had in my psilocybin nine teeners- the fevers of the sane in mushy prose- the health and safety of why gravity is gone. Here nor there this poem is a really trendy TV party- as if hearing song for a first time in a caprice of tactile spontaneous lust. The stars- the stars- what else but the stars and my unfulfilling job- and irregular jolts- coolly rekindling our ubiquitous camaraderie. I offer you the furrow in my brow and *Sarsaparilla*- scrub my face with dead fish- and recite this dinning bumble of conjecture to a class of hyper dreaming adolescent celebrities. The reclusive life is the myth I make for sake of some personal trauma. My gait is suffering. Implode forthwith in your groove.

3.16

I draw a breath upon which I mouth the word- pleasure. Her first pet was the Lion of Judah. This poem is a private enterprise. Intrepid- I communicated a truce between captive thoughts being tattooed on faces with nothing but a faulty torch and a failed zippo- I dwindled- I dwindled the devil's torque. I found my date in a sailor's hat- swaying- saying she was high to see me- since my last visit she's invested in an exotic aquarium. "Can't you see the devil orb of light?" To this I awakened to the rockabilly promoting plant food in the tavern. Someone says amen at the end of each freestyle a cappella- for the maiden's cream- the electric guitars.

3.17

The other girl of the world- a dumpy mass of atomic dumbness- says she's as game as any blue or white collar hussy. I'll soap a lather on my wrists to wash the light of my own path. Some days I simply tuned into birdsong. Some days I sleep as long as I can. It sucks that I can't afford a samurai sword- or her who straddled a hyper-intense invisible titan until climax. My love cavorts from neuron to neuron- know what I mean? The other poets bite our once endless night while we transcended a canvas of cloudless space. I had to look away- when I looked back it all seemed like I wanted to take a *Polaroid* of you both. If I took a mirror test to prove introverted epic frontiers and the thuds- the boke- then the same spake of the holy yoke is living off the kindness of strangers. Start throwing punches at my body for a fresh perspective. I love Christ. You can't blame me. It was only a theory. I won't know what to call this collagist opera. We chose a niche to stabilize our somatosensory slump. The end of… Then words are inscrutable in a convalescing perspective. Snorkelling you sing like the siskin on the birch branch. Of the eighties- when I'm bedridden- my eyes as my own- sometimes I would fall into becoming. If I re-write my CV with no mention of poetry- I'll audition for a thrash metal band- night's stellar winds blur this intensity of everything- I in my tin foil hat.

3.18

She loves you. Actions speak louder etc. Paranormal Investigator for delirium on the sea crest- give way on days of yore. My sallow propagator- like a plastic surgeon heeded no hindrance to her master plan for the pigtailed paraplegic- post-estranged in vitriolic flux she attacked us with her clutch bag. This ice age becomes a mere invention. At her beck I rested my full balls on the rim of the cold ceramic sink- while my impercipience sweats these daemons into ether- she reads aloud Turgenev. Betwixt this anal bleeding this wet dreaming- I'm all askew- languid in the quiet of your summer's midnights in which it was tight and tasted like nothing else- but- please these spates of fake rainbows of things to come. Qualify my flesh with the boundaries of our things to do schematic. Be both blood and guts. You'd no control of an Indian summer.

3.19

I stole a lime and a rose the second time I'd an out of body experience. Tenderness variant.
In this poem I'm dancing inside the head of a dreaming dog- mysterious flying objects incite
a vapid strangeness in my numskull. She played her trump in a medusoid response.
She gulps me like juice. I'm leaving a job like that of Christ. I don a bandana and burst
and float for a cause like death- I merge shadow and shadow into waves of respite grief-
a mesmerizing reverie- in which we talk toothaches- while you stitch holes in your pop socks-
fatigued by carbon footprints- your skirt rid up your thigh- I self reflexively propose- the fuck.

3.20

In your repaired pop socks- let's canoodle- make like our curfew is a nuisance caller or someone I could pretend is you- my love. My love is in your laugh which is a paper house of one another's poems- on fire with words that pretend the worst could happen- with nobody else to turn to- while watching kindred rejoice this comic apotheosis on a TV channel devoted ostensibly to true movies. I'm a hard grafter if put in charge of gods. Mean I say flunk in an intoned parodic voice.

3.21

Poetry- I'm sorry I took you somewhere more exotic than an induced hallucinosis- but he did not understand the hard words she began accounting for her faults. I say this a lot in vain. A crude motif. Like falling in love- as no one can with her realistically. The great gaping hole in the sky is ungodly. The neon visions of digital behemoths- I want to explore. I- a recent graduate like Crozier in the white Arctic with spittle I've been saving to douse you for pleasure's sake- selflessly- wearing an open bathrobe. When I propose a script of *Valium*- I text her off the cuff about love in times of too much info. Her walls of mirrors gave us back the broken image- how needs no why. We'd an impromptu spat for a nobody in particular. Fair enough to say that my white flag is romance rationed out to white cotton sport socks- to admonish aspirations between her vital centre. All my potential biographers suffer.

3.22

With junk food and wine the penis looked like a neglected pet that had come to lack
an orgasm by any means necessary. In the yearn and flash- otherwise incapacitated
for non-secular philistines- for the naif in me scrunching cartilage for plebeians- for bank
accounts- he would wash the quickening everything- punterless- not sure who stank- who
to make proud- the hairline crack of his heart maybe? A shimmying hand behind falls of hair?
The carcass of a rabbit? You're me when it comes to writing poems- at work stockpiling
limbs- or what he deems limbs- in a pair of pinstripe cotton boxers- sex starved. The clang
of my chimeric verve is obvious advice- I behest you need not prove its existence- I gust
my shy- trippy past into inoperable future skies- I've skitted peers of way back when- as if
prophecy of once upon a time- screw me for talk into lone nights in transit to break customary
silences of the ramshackle- whatever awaited them would be a knack of putting problems
in perspective. A fine curiosity altered the traffic- the crossing wires enmeshed in the fabric
of existential celibacy- of my objectivity- my immaturity of a lofty dream- and she said she was
hungry and sensitive and wanted to fetch me a whisky- your applause- vouch for the weather
in a pornographic biopic of my life- Venusian see-through thong at her heels- confirmed
in my mind the zombies responsible for road blocks- frig is it me or is this like some dream-
the way you nuzzle your exquisite noggin into your chest? Pillow talk and fake light- flowers
the walls of a padded cell- the glint of any weather incrementally chemical- still to gallivant-
interested in things like nothing is everything. When I walk I haven't got far to go as we drift-
as I drag this poem without the need of an umbrella and a hand grenade to get over myself-
or who's spun the most emotionally kaleidoscopic song. Sometimes I would read prose
and search for poetry that has the same energy and scope for light as that of the hiding sun.

3.23

#Postscript
I'm convivial.